A TRUE PATRIOTIC BEHIND THE INTEGRATION OF INDIA

BIOGRAPHY OF SHRI SARDAR VALLABHBHAI PATEL JI

SAINATH CHARY GANNOJI

Contents

PREFACE

Author's Preface:

During my schooling, I was not completely aware about the Iron Man of India but later in the year 2018 on 31st October, I came across a news article stating about the inauguration of Statue of Unity by our Honorable Prime Minister Shri Narendra Modi Ji at Vadodara, Gujarat. It was the event which have driven me to know more about Shri Sardar Vallabhbhai Patel. Heartfelt gratitude to our Hon'ble Prime Minister sir for such a great initiative through which a lot of YUVA have been seeking inspiration. Then after I was sad that why I haven't been taught since schooling about such great leader who strived to integrate India and started referring various resources and books available in government library which made me amaze to know about Sardar Vallabhbhai Patel's legacy and a thought provoked me to articulate the important life story of Sardar Patel into a book called *"A True Patriotic behind the Integration of India"*; So that every student can learn and seek inspiration from Sardar Ji's and can implicate his leadership values which will definitely make one self to drive them towards the progress of unity and integrity of the nation.

-*Sainath Chary Gannoji*

ACKNOWLEDGEMENTS

Author's Acknowledgement

Being a student I was constraint to have the space for working on this but by the grace of god, blessing and support of my parents and family I could able to refer various available resources in the government libraries and internet resources and I have penned down the important aspects of Sardar Patel Ji from those resources and also tried to mentioned about Shri VP Menon Ji in this book, because all the efforts made by Shri Sardar Vallabhbhai Patel Ji and VP Menon Ji will be a driving force for the generations of the nation to cherish the importance of the unity and spirit of integrity, I believe and will strive to distribute this book to all the students community, so that we as a future generation of the nation will be knowing about such great leaders who shed their efforts and time for the Nations Integrity!

I
PATEL'S CHILDHOOD

There was a middle-class agricultural family of Lewa Patidar community at Nadiad, Gujarat, British India.

On 31st October 1875 Vallabhbhai Jhaverbhai Patel who is famously known as Sardar Vallabhbhai Patel was the fourth son who have born to Shrimati Ladba Patel and Shri Jhaverbhai Patel.

Sardar Vallabhbhai Patel's father was the army personnel of the Rani Lakshmi of Jhansi while his mother was involved in spiritual activities. He was completely brought up in a Hindu Traditional Family, as he was a part of an agricultural family, he spent his childhood in the agricultural fields at Karamasad.

He started his Primary schooling at Karamasad and done High Schooling at Petlad, but he was mostly self-taught. After his schooling, he used to read law books by borrowing from others and cleared District Pleaders Examination. Patel was aimed to study the law in England, so he used to save his money for his Barrister Studies.

He got married to Jhaverba at the age of sixteen and was matriculated at the age of twenty-two i.e., in the year 1897. In the year 1900 Patel have started law practice at Godhra and after two years later he moved to Borsad with his wife and together they have setup a home and given birth to two children, with utmost dedication and hard work Mr. Patel had become capable lawyer. He distinguished himself as a lawyer in presenting an unassailable case with precise manner and in challenging police witnesses and British Judges. He also saved enough money to study law in England.

It was the day when Vallabhbhai Patel was a step away to achieve his dream to study law in England but fortunately or unfortunately he received a ticket for England with a name V.J Patel which was similar to his elder brother's initial ie; Vithalbhai Patel. So, Vithalbhai thought that the ticket was for him and at the same time Vallabhbhai Patel got to know that his elder brother is also interested to study in England. By knowing this he has sacrificed his England ticket to his brother in order to maintain his family's reputation.

Around 1908-1909 Patel's wife had serious health issues and have undergone a surgery but unfortunately, she didn't recover from it and left this world. On the same day he was engaged with a case discussion in a court and he received the news about the demise of his wife but he didn't leave the court until the completion of the case.

In the year 1910 i.e., at the age 36, Patel went to England to study law at the Middle Temple Inn. With his hard work and dedication, he has completed the course months earlier and also achieved the top place in Roman Law.

Patel travelled back to India in the year 1913 and established law practice at Ahmedabad, he was rising rapidly to become distinguished and leading barrister in Criminal Law at Ahmedabad bar.

He was reserved and courteous and remarked himself for his mannerism, western clothing style and meritorious champion in bridge at Ahmedabad's fashionable Gujarat Club.

Through this segment of his life, it reflects a quote which was written by Vallabhbhai Patel i.e.;

Faith is of no avail in absence of strength. Faith and Strength both are essential to accomplish any great work. -Sardar Vallabhbhai Patel

II

POLITICAL LIFE

Actually, Patel was nowhere interested in Politics but he was influenced by Mahatma Gandhi and changed his views when he met him in the year 1917.

It was the moment where Patel has inspired by Gandhi's Ideologies and became his follower.

Patel adhered to Gandhi's Policy of Nonviolence i.e., Satyagraha Movement and it led the way to struggle against the British.

In the year 1917 Patel have motivated the people of Borsad to join Gandhi's demand for Independence and Patel also joined the Indian National Congress Gujarat Sabha as secretary and helped in Gandhi's Campaigns.

In the year 1917, Patel was elected as the First Indian Sanitation Commissioner of Ahmedabad and served from 1917-1924.

As Patel started following Gandhi, he has changed his dressing style where he and his children burned their western clothing in fires and Boy Cott British Goods and started wearing Indian attire made of khadi and he has quit the Gujarat Club.

In the year 1918, Patel first made his mark by planning mass campaigns of peasants, farmers and land owners of Kaira, Gujarat against the decision of the Bombay Government to collect the full annual revenue taxes despite crop damage caused by heavy rains.

In the year 1923, Patel led the Satyagraha movement in Nagpur when Gandhi was in Prison but britishers have banned hoisting Indian Flag, Patel have succeeded in obtaining consent to hoist the flag publicly and also got the prisoners released.

From 1924-1928 Patel was elected and served as President of the Municipal Committee of Ahmedabad. During these years, he has implemented several Sanitation, Water Supply, administration and town planning programs. He also worked towards several Social Reforms, including Prohibition of Untouchability, Casteism, Alcoholism, etc.

In the year 1928, the government has raised the land revenue taxes when farmers of Bardoli Taluk, Surat District were already in trouble with famine Patel have visited every house and strengthened condition, before launching satyagraha movement, he have intimated all the villagers to maintain the non- violence and unity.

On February 12, 1928 the farmers refused to pay the taxes which were demanded by the government upon the call of Patel. Through this action government have responded by arresting farmers and confiscation their lands, even though farmers didn't give up. Various Satyagraha's were undertaken all over Gujarat to express solidarity and sympathy with Bardoli Farmers. The agitation continued for 6 months and Patel carried on his negotiation with the government. Through the leadership activities of Patel, the Government returned the seized lands to farmers and the postponement of implementation of increased taxes.

His efficient Leadership of Bardoli campaign earned him the title Sardar (leader) and he was also acknowledged as a Nationalist leader throughout India, but this recognized him as a dangerous enemy for British Government.

Gandhi gave the call for Dandi march and Salt Satyagraha to protest against the Salt Tax in the year 1930. Patel was one of the leaders who was supporting the moment was arrested before the Dandi march on 7th March 1930 and later Gandhi was also arrested which made the agitation intensified and demanded the release of two leaders by the public. In the month of June Patel was released from the prison and took charge as the Congress President in absence of Gandhi, but unfortunately, he was arrested once again.

In the year 1931 Patel was elected the President of the 46th session of the Indian National Congress at Karachi. Congress have approved the Gandhi-Irwin Pact, though Nehru and Bose have not agreed with the terms of the Pact. On the same day, Bhagat Singh and associates were executed in Lahore.

The Karachi session of the Congress have subsisted with a lot of turbulence. Thereafter, the India National Congress agreed to participate in the Round Table Conference in London. However, the conference didn't succeed but at subsequent time Patel, Gandhi and several other leaders were arrested.

From January 1931 to May 1933 Gandhi and Patel were kept in Yerwada Jail, but Gandhi protested against allocation of separate electorates for untouchables by starting fast-unto-death, Patel was looking after him. Later, he has been shifted to Nasik Jail for one year, and was released in 1934.

Patel have played an important role in raising funds and selecting candidates for the elections to provisional legislatures and also Patel have guided the ministers as the Chairman of the Congress Parliamentary Sub-Committee.

ॐ

Through this segment of his life, it reflects a quote which was written by Vallabhbhai Patel i.e.;

"By common endeavor we can rise the country to a new greatness, while a lack of unity will expose us to fresh calamities." – Sardar Vallabhbhai Patel

III

PATEL'S ROLE IN PARTITION OF INDIA

During the due course of time British Government have called for negotiations with the leaders of India for the Independence of the Nation, but the Muslim league leader Jinnah's separatist movement was the blockade Infront of the Indian Leaders.

Initially Patel was against the partition of India but in subsequent time he has changed his thought due to the communal conflicts which can lead to the weak government at the center, so due to these reasons he has agreed for creation of separate dominion which were based on religious preferences.

Gandhi and other leaders were against the Partition, but Patel had conversation with Gandhi and convinced him by conveying that the Congress-Muslim league alliance government may not work for the welfare of the people instead it can lead to a civil war in the country.

At the time of Independence, the partition of British India into India-Pakistan resulted in extensive communal riots. Patel have worked tirelessly to bring peace and provide the utmost safety and essentials to the refugees.

Patel have also visited border areas to organize various relief and setup refugee camps, he has also ordered South Indian army regiments to the bring the harsh situation under control.

Finally with utmost dedication and selfless sacrifices along with Sardar Vallabhbhai Patel and various other leaders the people of the nation got Independence.

Through this segment of his life, it reflects a quote which was written by Vallabhbhai Patel i.e.; ***"Every Indian should now forget that he is a Rajput, a Sikh or a Jat."*** –Sardar Vallabhbhai Patel

IV
GANDHI'S INFLUENCE ON PATEL

Gandhi's Principles and his life experiences had a huge effect on Patel's life. Patel have left his passion of Law practice by the Gandhi's call for the Non-Cooperation Movement and dedicated his life for the better and prosperous India. He stood with the Gandhi and followed Gandhi's path of nonviolence, as some of the Indian leaders used to not agree with the Gandhi's ideas but always Patel used to support and follow his ideas.

Through this segment of his life, it reflects a quote which was written by Vallabhbhai Patel i.e.;

"Non-violence has to be observed in thought, word and deed. The measure of our non-violence will be the measure of our success." - Sardar Vallabhbhai Patel

V

PATEL's SPEECH DURING INDEPENDENCE WEEK CELLEBRATIONS 1947

One of the speeches was given by Sardar Patel Ji

Sardar Ji delivered a speech on account of Independence week celebrations at one of the public gatherings on 11 August 1947 and I would like to quote few stances from that speech as follows;

Our first task is to Stabilise, Consolidate and Strengthen ourselves and the rest can have only a secondary priority. I appeal to you to rub out from your minds the memories of the *past two years, deem it as a terrible nightmare and forget it, and to look forward with single-minded purpose to make India strong, prosperous and happy. This can be done only by hard work. I am sure that all the Indian States will join the Indian Union and none can afford to keep out and live in isolation. First things should be done first and the first job is to get the states to accede to, and there by consolidate, the Union. In spite of my previous strong opposition to partition, I agreed to it because I felt convinced that in order to keep India united it must be divided now.*

– Sardar Vallabhbhai Patel

VI

WHO is VP MENON?

On September 30, 1893, Vappala Pangunni Menon was born in Ottapalam's tiny town of Panamanna, which is near to the banks of the Bharathapuzha. He was the oldest of a headmistress's twelve children. Finances were never easy with a family that big. Menon, who was then quite young, once overheard his father bemoaning the lack of finances and his inability to provide for his kids in the way they should have been.

The young child, who had barely completed his matriculation, was moved by his father's struggle to make ends meet and made the decision to forgo his education in favor of a series of low-paying jobs. He left his house in pursuit of employment with the goal of supporting his father financially and helping him.

He worked as a construction worker, a coal miner, a factory worker, a coolie-grade stoker, and even a failed cotton dealer. He did not restrict himself despite the strange occupations. He quickly accepted a position as a clerk-typist at a cigarette company with headquarters in Bangalore due to his ambition.

He was gifted with the English language and had a keen eye for problem-solving. The next thing he knew, he was on a plane to Shimla in search of employment with the government. Menon was able to secure a job as a clerk and typist in the home department in 1929 once he got there.

The British officials were fortunate to have him because of his quick and accurate typing. When he was moved to the Sensitive Reforms Department, Lord Linlithgow, the longest-serving Viceroy of India, made him a confidant.

Menon was not only trusted with access to sensitive material, but also served as a consultant on a number of reform choices. He frequently travelled to England with Linlithgow on business, making him the only local civil worker to attend the Roundtable Conference there at the time.

Menon was given the responsibility of serving as Lord Mountbatten's Political Reforms Commissioner in 1946. The British had agreed to grant India freedom, and the independence movement was at its height.

Menon was appointed secretary of the Ministry of the States in 1947 under Sardar Vallabhbhai Patel's leadership. His political acumen and hard ethic ensured that he would eventually become a strong ally of Patel.

Menon and Patel collaborated closely to bring more than 500 princely kingdoms into the Indian Union. His attempt to bargain with the young Maharaja of Jodhpur is one of the episodes that highlights the difficulty of the accession job.

Menon, who had accompanied Lord Mountbatten to the court, was tasked with persuading the king to ratify an interim arrangement of accession to the Indian Republic.

The Maharaja pulled out a fountain pen to sign the paper when Lord Mountbatten left and left Menon with him.

Menon was really taken aback when he realized the pen wasn't simply a pen. "After signing the document, he removed the cap to show a miniature 0.22 handgun, which he then pointed at Menon's head. He said, "I'm not heeding your threats." After hearing the noise, Mountbatten came back and took the gun. In addition to advised Patel on military action in the adversarial republics of Hyderabad and Junagadh, ties with Pakistan, and the Kashmir dispute, Menon utilized tact and diplomacy to persuade hesitant rulers to submit to India.

(I have referred various articles to present this context of great leader VP Menon Ji)

VII

EFFORTS AFTER INDEPENDENCE OF INDIA

Patel have been appointed as the first Deputy Prime Minister and the first Home Minister of Independent India. During the time British had given two options to the Princely States of India i.e., they could either join Pakistan or India or can stay as an independent country. This aspect has created a lot of precariousness situation in India.

As Patel was a home minister, he took up the responsibility and tirelessly tried to convince the Princely States to join in India.

With his tireless actions and insightful negotiations, successfully he has succeeded in integrating over 560 states to the Indian union. But unfortunately, few states like Junagadh, Jammu & Kashmir, & Hyderabad.

It could be difficult without these states to be as an Indian union and India would have been disjointed, Hence

Patel used his insightful thoughts and force to deal with them.

৪১

History Behind the Integration

In accordance with the Indian Independence Act of 1947, princely kingdoms had the choice of joining either Pakistan or India, or remaining a sovereign independent state.

At that time, there were more than 500 princely states, which together made up 28% of the population of pre-independent India and covered 48% of its land area.

Although these kingdoms technically did not belong to British India, they were totally obedient to the British Crown.

These nations served as the British Empire's essential allies, preventing the growth of rival colonial powers and Indian nationalist aspirations.

As a result, the princes received authority over their domains, but the British also gained the power to select ministers and request military assistance as needed.

The responsibility of merging the princely states was taken by Sardar Vallabhbhai Patel, India's first deputy prime minister and home minister, who took the aid of V.P. Menon, the secretary of the Ministry of the States.

Patel persisted in trying to persuade the princes to join India by appealing to their sense of patriotism and warning them of the potential for instability in the event of their refusal.

In addition, he created the idea of ***"privy purses,"*** which were payments paid to royal families in exchange for their consent to join with India.

The first states from Rajasthan to join the union were Bikaner, Baroda and several other states were adamant that they would not join India. Some of them believed that it was the ideal time to create an independent state, while others desired to join Pakistan.

Travancore

The maritime state in southern India was strategically located for maritime trade and had abundant mineral and people resources in Travancore.

One of the first princely states to reject joining the Indian union. In 1946, Sir C.P. Ramamswamy Aiyar, the Dewan of Travancore, announced his intention to form an independent state of Travancore that would be willing to enter into treaties with the Indian union, however latterly Travancore integrated into India on July 30, 1947.

Jodhpur

Despite having a Hindu king and a large Hindu population, the Rajput princely realm strangely had a lean towards Pakistan. Hanvant Singh, a young and new prince from Jodhpur, believed that because his realm bordered Pakistan, he may be able to negotiate a better "deal" with that nation.

According to reports, Jinnah gave the Maharaja a blank piece of paper on which he had written all of his requests. Along with military and agronomic support, he also promised him unrestricted access to the Karachi port for the production and importation of weapons.

When Patel realised the dangers of the border state joining Pakistan, he promptly got in touch with the prince and made a generous offer.

Patel reassured him that importing weapons would be permitted, that Jodhpur and Kathiawar would be connected by rail, and that India would provide grain to it in times of famine.

The State of Jodhpur was included into the Indian Dominion on August 11, 1947, when Maharaja Hanvant Singh, King of Jodhpur, signed the Instrument of Accession.

Bhopal

Bhopal was another state which claimed to be independent.

Here, Hamidullah Khan, a Muslim Nawab, ruled over a largely Hindu population who was a close associate of the Muslim League.

To Mountbatten, he had made it apparent that he intended to win independence.

But in response, the latter said that "no monarch could run away from the realm nearest to him."

When the Prince learned in July 1947 that many princes had joined India, he made the decision to do the same.

Hyderabad

It occupied a significant portion of the Deccan plateau and was the biggest and richest of all princely states.

In the princely state, Nizam Mir Osman Ali Khan was the last nizam ruler of Hyderabad which was predominated by Hindu population.

He boldly refused to join the Indian dominion and was extremely vocal in his demand for an independent state.

He attracted Jinnah's backing, and the conflict over Hyderabad intensified over time.

Requests and threats from Patel and other mediators did not sway the Nizam, who continued building up his army by bringing in weapons from Europe.

Armed extremists known as Razakars started using violence against Hyderabad's people, things started to become worse, following the June 1948 resignation of Lord Mountbatten.

Sardar Vallabhbhai Patel intruded by the "Operation Polo," Indian troops were dispatched to Hyderabad on September 13, 1948 for a police action. The Indian army took full control of the state after a four-day-long armed conflict, and Hyderabad was officially incorporated into India on 17/09/1948, which being celebrated now as a Hyderabad Liberation Day.

Junagadh

On the southwest corner of Gujarat, the princely state also resisted joining the Indian union by August 15, 1947.

It was the most significant of the Kathiawar kingdoms, had a sizable Hindu population, and was governed by Muhammad Mahabat Khanji III, the Nawab.

Despite Mountbatten's objections, Nawab Mahabat Khanji decided to join Pakistan on September 15, 1947, claiming that Junagadh was connected to it by sea.

Mangrol and Babariawad's rulers, two states under the suzerainty of Junagadh, responded by announcing their independence from Junagadh and joining India.

India refused to accept the Nawab's option of accession because it thought that allowing Junagadh to join Pakistan would exacerbate the already simmering communal tension in Gujarat.

The administration demanded a vote to determine the accession issue, citing the state's 80% Hindu population.

India cut off Junagadh's access to gasoline and coal, shut off air and land communications, put soldiers to the border, and invaded the princely states of Mangrol and Babariawad after they had become part of India.

Pakistan promised to talk about a vote in consideration for India withdrawing its soldiers, a demand that India rejected.

The Nawab and his family escaped to Pakistan on October 26 as a result of clashes with Indian troops. The Nawab had collected all of the money and assets from the state treasury before he left.

An election was held in February 1948, and India's admission received almost universal support.

Up to November 1, 1956, when Saurashtra was merged with Bombay state, Junagadh was a part of the Indian state of Saurashtra.

When Bombay state in which Junagadh was located was divided into the linguistic states of Maharashtra and Gujarat in 1960, Junagadh became a part of Gujarat state of India.

৪৩

Kashmir

It was a princely kingdom ruled by a Hindu king over a sizable Muslim majority that had resisted joining either of the two dominions. This kingdom's situation was not only exceedingly unique but also one of the hardest because it possessed crucial international borders.

Maharaja Hari Singh, the monarch of Kashmir, has proposed a cease-fire agreement to both India and Pakistan, pending a definitive decision regarding the state's membership.

Although Pakistan signed the standstill agreement, it invaded Kashmir from the north with a military force made up of soldiers and armed tribespeople. On October 24, 1947, thousands of tribal Pathan flooded into Kashmir in the early morning hours.

Jammu and Kashmir's Maharaja requested assistance from India. To request assistance from India, he sent his representative Sheikh Abdullah to Delhi.

Maharaja Hari Singh left Srinagar on October 26 and travelled to Jammu, where he signed the "Instrument of Accession" for the J&K state.

The establishment of an interim popular administration with Sheikh Mohammed Abdullah as prime minister was declared by Maharaja Hari Singh on March 5th, 1948.

The state constituent assembly was chosen in 1951. On October 31, 1951, it had its inaugural meeting in Srinagar.

The Delhi Agreement, which was signed in 1952 by the prime ministers of India and Jammu & Kashmir, granted the state unique status inside the Indian Constitutional framework.

The J&K Constituent Assembly approved the state's admission to the Union of India on February 6, 1954.

The Union Constitution was then extended to the state with a few exceptions and amendments by the President according to Article 370 of the Constitution.

The Constitution (Application to Jammu and Kashmir) Order, 2019, was issued on August 5 by the President of India.

The judgement effectively repeals the unique status granted to Jammu and Kashmir under Article 370.

Because of the Sardar Vallabhbhai Patel's tireless efforts, today we as an Indians are experiencing and exploring the different cultures with the thought of Unity in Diversity and India standed as the Integrated Nation.

ॐ

Through the efforts of Patel Ji, it reflects a quote which
was written by Vallabhbhai Patel i.e.;

*"Little pools of water tend to become stagnant and useless,
but if they are joined together to form a big lake the
atmosphere is cooled and there is universal benefit."*

– Sardar Vallabhbhai Patel

VIII

SARDAR PATEL'S DEMISE

Unfortunately, in the year 1948 Patel have suffered a heart-attack by knowing the Gandhi's assassination and health began to worsen in the mid half of 1950.

On December 15, 1950 Patel have left the life at the age of 75 in the Bombay by this entire nation as saddened and moured.

On the day of 15 December 1950, the Parliament was assembled in New Delhi an hour later to the Patel's Death and the Prime Minister Nehru announced his lost to the house.

During the meeting Nehru stated Patel is the 'Builder and Consolidator of New India.

IX

PATELS LEGACY

In the year 1980, the Sardar Patel National memorial was opened at Moti Shahi Mahal, Ahmedabad.

The International airport in Ahmedabad & several academic institutions are named after Patel.

In the state of Gujarat, a major dam on River Narmada was dedicated to Patel and named it as Sardar Sarovar Dam.

In the year 1991, Patel was awarded with India's highest Civilian Award, Bharat Ratna Award.

In the year 2014, under the Leadership of our PM sir Narendra Modi, Government of India have announced that nation would annually celebrate Patel's birthday as Rashtriya Ekta Diwas/ National Unity Day on 31 October 2014.

On 31st October 2018, PM sir shri Narendra Modi ji has inaugurated the Statue of Unity and dedicated to Sardar Vallabhbhai Patel.

Statue of Unity is one of the world's tallest statue which is approximately 182 meters in height.

Statue of Unity is located at Vadodara, Gujarat. The entire complex is surrounded by an artificial lake and it became the one of the most popular tourist places in India.

Authors Conclusion

Sardar Vallabhbhai Patel was the main pillar and reason for the Unification of India and his life story clearly reveals that our beloved Sardar Vallabhbhai Patel is the *Iron Man of India*, I feel it as an opportunity to articulate the context of True Patriotic behind the Integration of the India, through which a lot of yuva (youth) like me could seek inspiration to spread the unity and spirit of integrity! Jai Bharat!

31 October, 2018 was the day which motivated me to know about the Sardar Vallabhbhai Patel, on this note I would like to convey my thanks to PM Narendra Modi Ji for leading the nation to prosper and inculcate patriotism with his insightful initiatives.

– Sainath Chary Gannoji